MEETING
THE NIGHT

MEETING THE NIGHT

*Bedtime Prayers
and Meditations from
Around the World*

Brian Wright

Adams Media Corporation
HOLBROOK, MASSACHUSETTS

Published by
Adams Media Corporation
260 Center Street, Holbrook, MA 02343

ISBN: 1-58062-120-1

Printed in the United States of America.

J I H G F E D C B A

Library of Congress Cataloging-in-Publication Data

Meeting the night: bedtime prayers and meditations from around
the world / [compiled by] Brian Wright.
        p.   cm.
      ISBN 1-58062-120-1
    1. Prayers. I. Wright, Brian.
      BL560.M44   1999
  291.4'33—dc21   98-31839
                  CIP

Cover Illustration:
The Starry Night Over Rhone/Vincent Van Gogh/Super Stock.

This book is available at quantity discounts for bulk purchases.
For information, call 1-800-872-5627 (in Massachusetts, 781-767-8100).

Visit our home page at http://www.adamsmedia.com

Table of Contents

Foreword

SURRENDERING OURSELVES TO THE FORCES OF
SLEEP IS MORE THAN JUST AN ACQUIESCENCE TO
OUR BODIES' PROPERTIES OF REJUVENATION. It
can be a spiritual connection to the world, a
sacred ritual, a personal communion with God.

The ancients of many cultures were very
aware of the microcosmic death and rebirth
that each night of sleep held in store for
them. Many of their prayers and their
conversations with God marked this
passage into the unconscious world. Some
of the best of these ancient prayers are
included here.

If we observe our children or remember
back to our own childhoods, we see the
wonder and sometimes the fear that are
innate parts of our daily existence. These

emotions have been eloquently expressed by innocent, wise children throughout the world in original prayers of their own. The voices of these children speak from the pages of this book.

Wisdom, of course, is not limited to the ancient and the innocent. Our modern-day thinkers, philosophers, and sages have also created some of the most moving prayers for closing the day and opening the mysteries of night. This book presents a number of these voices as well.

The prayers and meditations in this anthology are refreshingly eclectic. They are filled with awe and laden with humor. They are written by ancient mystics, modern-day thinkers, and small children. They represent many of the religions and cultures of our world. They are all worthy of your study, reflection, and meditation. Many of the shorter entries are intended as starting points for further contemplation and meditation.

I offer this collection of bedtime prayers and meditations not only to share the insight and wisdom of people of all ages, cultures, and religions but also to show the commonality of our connection to God.

The entries in this anthology were selected from holy texts, works by contemporary writers, historical and religious archives, and poetry collections. I hope that you find it useful and inspiring—and that it moves you to meet the night more peacefully.

Brian Wright

Gratitude

1

I called out to you,
and you came to my aid
in your own way—
a way that sometimes carries laughter,
and other times brings tears.
Yet, it's all in accordance
with your great cosmic plan.

—BRIAN WRIGHT

2

Night is drawing nigh.
For all that has been — Thanks!
For all that shall be — Yes!

—DAG HAMMARSKJÖLD

3

And now I wish to pray and perform
a ritual of my devotion to the sun.
I will bow and sing beneath my breath,
then perform the dance of farewell
and my confidence in the sun's return.
All is dance;
the sun glides along the horizon;
now the leaves sway;
now the Earth spins.

—DAVID IGNATOW

4

*I reverently speak in the presence
of the great parent God:
I give Thee grateful thanks
that Thou hast enabled me to live this day,
the whole day,
in obedience to the excellent spirit
of Thy ways.*

—SHINTO PRAYER

5

May the moon rise well!
May the earth appear
brightly shone upon.

—Sioux song

6

I will celebrate Thy praise,
Lord of Heaven and Earth,
when I rise up,
and praise Thee
in the night season,
and when the stars
begin to disappear.

—ADAPTED FROM THE KORAN

7

*And the night of darkness
and the dawn of light,
meeting, joining one another,
helpmates ever, they.
All is beautiful,
all is beautiful,
all is beautiful, indeed.*

—From the Navajo Song of the Earth

8

Be with us, Lord.
We have joy, we have joy.
When I awake,
I am still with you.

—CELTIC NIGHT PRAYER

9

In the peace of night I worship Thee.
The sunlight that revealed
a myriad earthly allurements has vanished.
One by one I shut the doors of my senses,
lest the fragrance of the rose
or the song of the nightingale
distract my love from Thee.
Like night, I adore Thee
in hiddenness and silence.
Within the shrine of darkness
I invoke Thee, Blessed and Beloved!

—PARAMAHANSA YOGANANDA

10

Blessed art Thou, Lord our God,
King of the universe,
who with His word brings on the evenings,
with wisdom opens the gates,
with understanding alters the phases,
varies the seasons,
and arranges the stars in their heavenly
orbit according to His will.
He creates day and night.
He rolls away the light from
before the darkness and the darkness
from before the light,
He makes the day to pass
and the night to come,
and divides between day and night;
Lord of hosts is His name.

A living and everlasting God,
who shall constantly reign over us
forever and ever.
Blessed art Thou Lord,
who brings on the evenings.

— TRADITIONAL JEWISH PRAYER

11

I love to watch the twinkling stars appear—
Like lanterns freshly trimmed,
they light the sky—
Each comes to its appointed place to guard
the Earth, like silent sentinels on high.
They draw a purple mantle over all
to hide from view the dome
of daylight blue,
assuring man that dawn will surely bring
God's holy hour to start each day anew.
And while the Earth is wrapped
in peaceful sleep,
the soul is borne away on beams of light,
inspired, sanctified by heaven's host;
ah, mystic night—
enchanted, dreamland night!

—ELEANOR FLOCK

12

Ah, so soon you'd leave me pining?
Winks ago you seemed so near!
Banks of clouds conceal your shining,
Now you are no longer here.
But you feel how I am saddened
When your brim is like a star,
Proving that I should be gladdened
By a love, however far.
Rise with bright and brighter glamour
On your course in splendor dight!
Harder though my sick heart hammer,
Yet, how blissful is the night.

—GOETHE

13

*Glory be to God
when ye enter the night
and when ye enter the morning.
Unto Him be praises
in the heavens and the Earth,
and at the sun's decline
and in the noonday.*

—THE KORAN

14

In the great night my heart will go out,
Towards me the darkness comes rattling,
In the great night my heart will go out.

—TEWA SONG

15

O resplendent night,
may you lead us sinless
to dawn,
from dawn to day,
and from day back to you!

—ATHARVA-VEDA

16

Thank you, God,
for the day and its work
and the night and its rest.

—FROM *THANK YOU, GOD!*
  A JEWISH CHILD'S BOOK OF PRAYERS

Protection

17

God, my friend,
I'm going to need you to help me
in my sleep tonight.
I ask that you carry me swiftly
across the threshold of consciousness
into the world of my dreams.
And while I'm away
on my soul's journey,
guard my body and my home.

—BRIAN WRIGHT

18

Be present, O merciful God,
and protect us through the silent hours
of this night,
so that we who are wearied
by the changes and chances
of this fleeting world
may rest upon Thy eternal changelessness.

—AN ANCIENT COLLECT AT COMPLINE

19

So favor us this night,
O Thou whose pathways we have visited
as birds who nest upon a tree.
Night hath put all her glories on;
the villagers who sought their homes,
and all that walks and all that flies.
Keep wolf and thief away;
from falling lightnings keep us safe
great King of all the mighty world.

—THE RIG-VEDA

20

The night falls
The hills are black
And the sky resembles a rainbow
In which the white moon swims.
I, sitting under the stars in the cold,
Think about my life and of the future.
The stars are the eyes of the night
And they see all . . .
But I feel that I am blind.

—KIRSTEN SAVITRI BERGH,
   TRANSLATED BY DAVID GALLARDO

2 1

God, save us.
God, hide us.
When we sleep, God do not sleep.
If we sleep, God do not get drowsy.
Tie us around Your arm, God,
like a bracelet.

—SAMBURU PRAYER, KENYA

22

Lord, tender shepherd, hear me;
bless Your little lamb tonight;
through the darkness please be near me;
keep me safe till morning light.
All this day Your hand has led me,
and I thank You for Your care;
You have warmed and clothed and fed me;
listen to my evening prayer.

—ORIGIN UNKNOWN

23

Lord and God of power,
shield and sustain me this night,
Lord, God of power,
this night and every night.
Sain and deliver me from fault,
sain and deliver me from sin,
sain my soul and my body,
each dark and each light.
Bless to me the land whither I am bound,
bless to me the thing my eye shall see,
bless to me the thing my purpose discerns,
God of life, bless my condition.
Bless the journey whereon I go,
bless the earth that is under my foot,
bless the matter which I seek,
King of glory, bless my condition.

—CELTIC PRAYER

24

Now I will sleep beneath your feet,
beneath your hands,
O Lord of the mountains and valleys,
O Lord of the trees,
O Lord of the creeping vines.
Again tomorrow there will be day,
again tomorrow there will be light.
I know not where I will be.
Who is my mother? Who is my father?
Only you, O God.
You watch me, guard me, on every path,
through every darkness,
and before each obstacle that you might
hide or take away, O God, my Lord,
O Lord of the mountains and valleys.

My words, my thoughts, are these.
I may have said too much,
or not enough.
You will endure, you will forgive
my error.

—KEKCHI MAYA

25

Thou whose nature cannot sleep,
On my temples sentry keep;
Guard me against those watchful foes,
Whose eyes are open while mine close.
Let no dreams my head infest,
But such as Jacob's temples blessed.
While I do rest, my soul advance,
Make my sleep a holy trance.
That I may, my rest being wrought,
Awake into some holy thought.
And with as active vigor run,
My course, as does the nimble sun.

—SIR THOMAS BROWN

26

Thou Being of marvels,
Shield me with might,
Thou Being of statutes
And of stars.
Compass me this night,
Both soul and body,
Compass me this night
And on every night.
Compass me aright
Between earth and sky,
Between the mystery of Thy laws
And mine eye of blindness;
Both that which mine eyes sees
And that which it reads not;
Both that which is clear
And is not clear to my devotion.

—ANCIENT GAELIC PRAYER

27

The day is past, the sun is set,
and the white stars are in the sky;
while the long grass with dew is wet,
and through the air the bats now fly.
The lambs have now lain down in sleep,
the birds have long since
sought their nests;
the air is still; and dark, and deep
on the hillside the old wood rests.
Yet of the dark I have no fear,
but feel as safe as when 'tis light;
for I know God is with me there,
and He will guard me through the night.

For God is by me when I pray,
and when I close mine eyes in sleep,
I know that He will with me stay,
and will all night watch by my keep.
For He who rules the stars and sea,
who makes the grass and trees to grow,
will look on a poor child like me,
when on my knees I to Him bow.
He holds all things in His right hand,
the rich, the poor, the great, the small;
when we sleep, or sit, or stand,
is with us, for He loves us all.

—THOMAS MILLER

28

*The angels of God guard us
through the night,
and quieten the powers of darkness.
The spirit of God be our guide
to lead us to peace and to glory.
It is but lost labor that we haste
to rise up early,
and so late take rest,
and eat the bread of anxiety.
For those beloved of God are given gifts
even while they sleep.*

—NEW ZEALAND PRAYER BOOK

29

With all her eyes the goddess Night
looks forth approaching many a spot:
She hath put all her glories on.
Immortal, she hath filled the waste,
the goddess hath filled height and depth:
She conquers darkness with her light.
The goddess as she comes hath set
the Dawn her sister in her place:
and then the darkness vanishes.
So favor us this night,
O thou whose pathways we have visited
as birds their nest upon the tree.
The villagers have sought their homes,
and all that walks and all that flies,
even the falcons fain for prey.

Keep off the she-wolf and the wolf;
O night, keep the thief away:
Easy be thou for us to pass.
Clearly hath she come nigh to me
who decks the dark with richest hues:
O morning, cancel it like debts.
These have I brought to the like kine.
O night, thou child of heaven,
accept this laud for a conqueror.

—THE RIG-VEDA

30

We wait in the darkness!
Come, all ye who listen,
help in our night journey.
Now no sun is shining;
Now no star is glowing;
Come show us the pathway;
The night is not friendly;
The moon has forgot us,
we wait in the darkness!

—IROQUOIS PRAYER

31

O God, my guardian,
stay always with me.
In the morning,
in the evening,
by day,
or by night,
always be my helper.

—POLISH PRAYER

32

O God do Thou Thine ear incline,
protect my children and my kine,
even if Thou art weary, still forbear
and harken to my constant prayer.
When shrouded beneath the cloak of night,
the splendors of sleep beyond our sight,
and when the sky by day,
Thou movest, still to Thee I pray,
dread shades of our departed sires,
Ye who can make or mar desires,
slain by no mortal hand ye dwell,
beneath the Earth, O guard us well.

—NANDI PRAYER, KENYA

33

Lord, when we sleep
let us not be made afraid,
but let our sleep be sweet,
that we may be enabled
to serve Thee on the morrow.

—WILLIAM LAUD

34

Preserve us, O God, while waking,
and guard us while sleeping,
that awake we may watch with God,
and asleep we may rest in Your peace.

—New Zealand Prayer Book

35

The sacred Thee
To save
To shield
To surround
The hearth
The house
The household
This eve
This night
O! This eve
This night
And every night
Each single night.

—GAELIC PRAYER

36

Dear God,
as a hen covers her chicks
with her wings
to keep them safe,
do Thou this dark night protect us
under Your golden wings.

—PRAYER, INDIA

37

Lord, let Your light be only for the day,
and the darkness for the night.
And let my dress, my poor humble dress
lie quietly over my chair at night.
Let the church bells be silent,
my neighbor Ivan not ring them at night.
Let the wind not waken the children
out of their sleep at night.
Let the hen sleep on its roost,
the horse in the stable
all through the night.
Remove the stone
from the middle of the road
that the thief may not stumble at night.

Let heaven be quiet during the night,
restrain the lightning, silence the thunder,
they should not frighten mothers
giving birth to their babies at night.
And me too protect against fire and water,
protect my poor roof at night.
Let my dress, my poor humble dress
lie quietly over my chair at night.

—Nahum Bomze

38

Save us while waking,
and defend us while sleeping,
that when we awake
we may watch with God,
and when we sleep
we may rest in peace.

—ANTIPHON AT COMPLINE

39

Good night! Good night!
Far flies the light;
but still God's love
shall flame above,
making all bright.
Good night! Good night!

—VICTOR HUGO

Comfort

40

God, my friend,
I need you to ease my hurt and harm tonight.
I ask that you find the source of my pain,
and bathe that place
with your unconditional love.
Help me to remember that
pain and suffering are essential parts
of being human.

—BRIAN WRIGHT

41

*In faith let us beseech the Lord
that we may pass in peace the evening
that is drawing nigh
and the night that is to come.*

—ANCIENT ARMENIAN LITURGY

42

Heavenly Father, as people turn to sleep,
please bless all those who
cannot sleep tonight.
Comfort those who are sad.
Forgive those who have done wrong.
Calm those who are worried.
Help those who are in pain.
And grant Your peace
to every troubled heart.

—ORIGIN UNKNOWN

43

The sun descending in the west,
The evening star does shine
The birds are silent in their nest,
And I must seek for mine.

—WILLIAM BLAKE

44

Now that evening has fallen,
to God, the Creator,
I will turn in prayer,
knowing that He will help me,
I know the Father will help me.

—DINKA PRAYER, SUDAN

45

Abide with me.
Fast falls the eventide;
The darkness deepens;
Lord, with me abide;
When other helpers fail,
and comforts flee,
Help of the helpless,
O abide with me.

—HENRY FRANCIS LYTE

46

Where in the galaxy
does it wait
my wandering star?

—LUCIEN STRYK

47

Deep peace, pure white of the moon to you.
Deep peace, pure green of the grass to you.
Deep peace, pure brown of the earth to you.
Deep peace, pure grey of the dew to you.
Deep peace, pure blue of the sky to you.
Deep peace, of the running wave to you.
Deep peace, of the flowing air to you.
Deep peace, of the quiet earth to you.
Deep peace, of the shining stars to you.
Deep peace, of the Son of peace to you.

—FIONA MCCLEOD

48

O God, you have let me pass this day in peace,
let me pass the night in peace
O Lord who has no Lord,
there is no strength but in Thee.
Thou alone hast no obligation.
Under Thy hand I pass the night.
Thou art my mother and my father.

—BORAN PRAYER, KENYA

49

*As my head rests on my pillow
Let my soul rest in Your mercy.
As my limbs relax on my mattress,
Let my soul relax in Your peace.
As my body finds warmth
beneath the blankets,
Let my soul find warmth in Your love.
As my mind is filled with dreams,
Let my soul be filled
with visions of heaven.*

—JOHANN FREYLINGHAUSEN

50

Goodnight God.
I hope you are having
a good time being the world.
I like the world very much.
I'm glad you made the plants
and trees survive with the
rain and summers.
When summer is nearly near
the leaves begin to fall.
I hope you have a good time
being the world.
I like how God feels around
everyone in the world.
God, I am very happy that
I live on you.

Your arms clasp around the world.
I like you and your friends.
Every time I open my eyes
I see the gleaming sun.
I like the animals — the deer,
and us creatures of the world,
the mammals.
I love my dear friends.

—DANU BAXTER, AGE $4^1/_2$

51

Watch, dear Lord,
with those who wake, or watch,
or weep tonight,
and give Your angels charge
over those who sleep.
Tend Your sick ones, O Lord God,
rest Your weary ones.
Bless Your dying ones.
Soothe Your suffering ones.
Pity Your afflicted ones.
Shield Your joyous ones.
And all for Your love's sake,
Amen.

—ST. AUGUSTINE

52

Come, Lord,
and cover me with the night.
Spread Your grace over us
as You assured us You would do.
Your promises are more than
all the stars in the sky;
Your mercy is deeper than the night.
Lord, it will be cold.
The night comes with its breath of death.
Night comes; the end comes; You come.
Lord, we wait for You
day and night.

— PRAYER, GHANA

53

I am going now into sleep,
be it that I in health shall wake;
If death be to me in deathly sleep,
Be it that in Thine own arm's keep,
O God of grace, to new life I wake;
O be it in Thy dear arm's keep,
O God of grace, that I shall awake!

—POEM, WESTERN HIGHLANDERS

54

*May he who brings
flowers tonight
have moonlight.*

— KIKAKU

55

Bless, O God, this dwelling,
and each who rests herein this night;
Bless, O God, my dear ones
in every place wherein they sleep;
In the night that is tonight,
and every single night;
In the day that is today,
and every single day.

—CELTIC PRAYER

56

God, that madest earth and heaven,
darkness and light:
who the day for toil has given
for rest the night:
may Thine angel-guards defend us,
slumber sweet Thy mercy send us,
holy dreams and hopes attend us,
this livelong night.

—BISHOP REGINALD HEBER

57

Now that the sun has set,
I sit and rest, and think of You.
Give my weary body peace.
Let my legs and arms stop aching,
let my nose stop sneezing,
let my head stop thinking.
Let me sleep in your arms.

—TRADITIONAL DINKA PRAYER, SUDAN

58

The night is here.
Be near to me, dear Lord.
Be a bright candle shining in the dark,
driving the sin from my heart.
The day will come.
Hasten the dawn, dear Lord.
Hasten the time when
the sun of righteousness
shines into the depths of my heart.
The Moon casts her gentle rays.
Guide me, dear God.
Guide my steps through this gloomy path
that I may arrive safely in heaven.
The stars glisten in the sky.

Teach me, dear God,
Teach me to discern the truth
amidst falsehood,
That even now I may see signs
of Your glory.

—JOHANN FREYLINGHAUSEN

59

Lord of light
help me to know
that You are also
Lord of night.
And by Your choice
when all is dark
and still and stark
You use Your voice.

—Harry Alfred Wiggett

60

Lord God, light unfailing,
Creator of all lights
and Sun of this whole world,
bless now the lighting
of this evening lamp;
a symbol of Your purity and radiance
and a token of Your presence
and Your power.

—LITURGY OF JYOTINIKETAN COMMUNITY

61

*Let me wake in the night
and hear it raining
and go back to sleep.*

—WENDELL BERRY

62

O Lord, support us all the day long,
until the shadows lengthen,
and the evening comes,
and the busy world is hushed,
and the fever of life is over,
and our work is done.
Then in Your mercy,
grant us a safe lodging,
and a holy rest,
and peace at the last.

—BOOK OF COMMON PRAYER

Rejuvenation

63

God, my friend,
I need you to recharge
my exhausted being
with your infinite supply of energy.
You are the sun behind the sun—
the ultimate power supply
for spirit, soul, and matter.
I cannot help but accept
your rejuvenating breath,
for it is the very breath of all life.

—BRIAN WRIGHT

64

As the day ends
and the shadows of night fall,
we pray that our sleep is peaceful,
filled with pleasant dreams.
May we awaken rested
and ready for a new day.

—From *Thank You, God! A Jewish Child's*
  Book of Prayers

65

Sweet spirit of sleep,
who brings peace and rest to weary bodies,
empty us of aches and pains,
for we struggle as seeds through
unyielding earth.
Bring to us the timeless nature
of Your presence—
the endless void of our slumber.
Make us aware of the work we can do
while in Your time,
make us to know Your dreaming,
where past and future are reconciled.

Come let us honor sleep,
that knits up the raveled sleeve of care,
the death of each day's life,
sore labor's bath,
balm of hurt minds,
great nature's second course,
chief nourisher in life's feast.

—CONGREGATION OF ABRAXAS

66

The sun has disappeared.
I have switched off the light,
and my wife and children are asleep.
The animals in the forest are full of fear,
and so are the people on their mats.
They prefer the day with Your sun
to the night.
But I still know that Your moon is there,
and Your eyes and also Your hands.
Thus I am not afraid.
This day again
You led us wonderfully.
Everybody went to his mat
satisfied and full.

Renew us during our sleep,
that in the morning
we may come afresh to our daily jobs.
Be with our brothers far away in Asia
who may be getting up now. Amen.

—PRAYER, GHANA

67

O Lord God, refresh us
with quiet sleep
when we are wearied
with the day's labor,
that,
being assisted with the help
which our weakness needs,
we may be devoted to Thee
both in body and mind.

—LEONINE SACRAMENTARY,
   FIFTH CENTURY

68

Glory to you, my God, this night,
For all the blessings of the light,
To you, from whom all good does come,
Our life, our health, our lasting home.
Teach me to live, that I may dread
The grave as little as my bed,
Teach me to die, that so I may
Rise glorious at the aweful day.
O may I now on you repose,
And may kind sleep my eylids close,
Sleep that may me more vigorous make
To serve my God when I awake.
If I lie restless on my bed,
Your word of healing peace be said,
If powerful dreams rise in the night,
Transform their darkness into light.

—NEW ZEALAND PRAYER BOOK

69

*In the night of weariness
let me give myself up to sleep
without struggle,
resting my trust upon Thee.
Let me not force my flagging spirit
into a poor preparation for Thy worship.
It is Thou who drawest the veil of night
upon the tired eyes of the day
to renew its sight in a fresher gladness
of awakening.*

—RABINDRANATH TAGORE

70

O Lord God,
who has given us the night for rest,
I pray that in my sleep
my soul may remain awake to You,
steadfastly adhering to Your love.
As I lay aside my cares to relax
and relieve my mind,
may I not forget Your infinite
and unresting care for me.
And in this way,
let my conscience be at peace,
so that when I rise tomorrow,
I am refreshed in body, mind and soul.

—JOHN CALVIN

71

Oh, Life of Life, the light
Thou art to me of day,
the dark of night.
Relieve me of my vice and virtue;
make my heart void,
and this heart made empty fill
with Thy entirety.

—C. R. DAS

72

Now the day is over,
night is drawing nigh,
shadows of the evening
steal across the sky.
Now the darkness gathers,
stars begin to peep,
birds and beasts and flowers
soon will be asleep.
Lord, give the weary
calm and sweet repose;
with Thy tenderest blessing
may our eyelids close.

Grant to little children
visions bright of Thee;
guard the sailors tossing
on the deep blue sea.
When the morning wakens,
then may I arise,
pure, and fresh, and sinless
in Thy holy eyes.

—SABINE BARING-GOULD

73

*At night make me one
with the darkness,
in the morning
make me one with the light.*

—WENDELL BERRY

74

Take us, we pray Thee,
oh Lord of our life,
into Thy keeping
this night and forever.
O Thou light of lights,
keep us from inward darkness.
Grant us so to sleep in peace
that we may rise to work
according to Thy will.

—BISHOP LANCELOT ANDREWES

75

Lord, with Your praise
we drop off to sleep.
Carry us through the night,
make us fresh for the morning.
Hallelujah for the day!
And blessing for the night!

—FISHERMAN'S PRAYER, GHANA

76

When starry worlds
Transplant my sleeping I
Into the land of Spirit,
I will draw strength of soul
From World-creative Powers
To strive toward the Spirit.

—RUDOLF STEINER

77

O Lord God,
the life of mortals, the light of the faithful,
the strength of those who labor
and the repose of the dead;
grant us a tranquil night
free from all disturbance;
that after an interval of quiet sleep,
we may, by Thy bounty,
at the return of light be endowed
with activity from the Holy Spirit
and enabled in security
to render thanks to Thee.

—FROM THE MOZARABIC LITURGY

78

Let our sleeping soul remember,
and be awake and be alive,
in contemplation,
of how our life passes away,
of how our death comes forward to us,
so silently.

—JORGE MANRIQUE

79

O God, who gives the day for work
and the night for sleep,
refresh our bodies and our minds
through the quiet hours of night,
and let our inward eyes
be directed towards You,
dreaming of your eternal glory.

— LEONINE SACRAMENTARY,
  FIFTH CENTURY

80

O Lord,
who received the children
who came to you,
receive also from me, your child,
this evening prayer.
Shelter me under the shadow
of your wings,
that in peace I may lie down and sleep;
and waken me in due time,
that I may glorify you. . . .

—EASTERN ORTHODOX PRAYER

81

I go to sleep.
Till I awaken,
my soul will be in the spiritual world,
and will there meet the higher Being
who guides me through this earthly life —
Him who is ever in the spiritual world,
who hovers above my head.
My soul will meet Him,
ever the guiding Genius of my life.
And when I awaken again
this meeting will have been.
I shall have felt the wafting of his wings.
The wings of my Genius
will have touched my soul.

—RUDOLF STEINER

82

I thank You, O God,
for Your care and protection this day,
keeping me from harm
and spiritual corruption.
I now place the work of the day
into Your hands,
trusting that You will redeem my errors
and turn my achievements to Your glory.
And I now ask You to work within me,
trusting that You will use the hours
of rest to create in me a new heart
and new soul.
Let my mind, which through the day
has been directed to my work,
through the evening be wholly directed
at You.

—JAKOB BOEHME

83

I'm tired, Lord,
but I'll lift one foot
if you'll lift the other
for me.

—SADIE PATTERSON

Release

84

God, my friend,
take me away
to the place of letting go.
Help me to forgive,
and to give up those things
that keep me stuck,
so that I may learn to receive
through the sacred act of giving away.

—BRIAN WRIGHT

85

In an accessible place
you will sleep.
At midnight,
I will come.

—INCA SONG

86

The moon in the pines
Now I hang it up, now I take it off
And still I keep gazing.

—ANONYMOUS HAIKU

87

Now, into the keeping of God I put
all doings of today.
All disappointments,
hindrances,
forgotten things,
negligences.
All gladness and beauty,
love,
delight,
achievement.
All that people have done for me,
All that I have done for them,
my work and my prayers.

And I commit all the people whom I love
to His shepherding,
to His healing and restoring,
to His calling and making.

—MARGARET CROPPER

88

Where the sun sets,
The Holy Young Woman
The cliff rose arrow
Has swallowed
And withdrawn it.
The moon
Is satisfied.

—AMERICAN INDIAN SONG

89

Lord, a look from You can embrace us
with peaceful sleep,
and ensure that our dreams
are pure and holy.
Sin shudders and falters
at Your glance,
and guilt dissolves into tears
of repentance.
Bring peace, Lord, to our weary minds,
and give rest to our tired limbs.
May we leave sin behind us,
and may our final reflections
before sleep be prayers
for Your mercy.

—BISHOP LANCELOT ANDREWES

90

The river is smooth and calm this evening.
The spring flowers bloom.
The moon floats on the current.
The tide carries the stars.

—EMPEROR YANG OF SUI

91

I don't like the man who doesn't sleep,
    says God.
Sleep is the friend of man.
Sleep is the friend of God.
Sleep is perhaps the most beautiful thing
I have created.
And I myself rested on the seventh day.
He whose heart is pure, sleeps.
And he who sleeps has a pure heart.

—CHARLES PEGUY

92

In the night of weariness
let me give myself up to sleep
without struggle,
resting my trust upon Thee.
Let me not force my flagging spirit
into a poor preparation for Thy worship.
It is Thou who drawest the veil of night
upon the tired eyes of the day
to renew its sight
in a fresher gladness of awakening.

—SADHU SUNDAR SINGH

93

When day is letting go,
the mind may follow too,
and what we could not find by light,
the dark may bring to view.
The words that would not come,
the phrases never found,
present themselves at night:
perfect, obvious,
right in sense and sound.

—THOMAS TROEGER

94

Day is done.
Gone the sun.
From the lake,
from the hills,
from the sky.
All is well,
safely rest.
God is nigh.

— "Taps,"
LYRICS BY GENERAL DANIEL BUTTERFIELD

95

How tender the heart grows
at the twilight hour,
more sweet seems the perfume
of the sunless flower.
Come quickly, wings of night,
the twilight hurts too deep.
Let darkness wrap the world around,
my pain will go to sleep.

—UNA H. MARSON

96

*One sunset hour
wrapped in sacrificial fire
then I shall enter Thee,
spirit of all sands,
and Thy night
will cool my small desire
to be among my kinsmen.*

—EDA LOU WALTON

97

Twilight is a time for sharing—
and a time for remembering—
sharing the fragrance
of the cooling earth—
the shadows of the gathering dusk—
Here our two worlds meet and pass—
the frantic sounds of man grow dimmer
as the light recedes—
the unhurried rhythm of the other world
swells in volume as the darkness deepens—
It is not strange that discord has no place
in this great symphony of sound—
it is not strange that a sense of peace

descends upon all living things—
it is not strange that memories
burn more brightly—
as the things of substance
lose their line and form
in the softness of the dark—
Twilight is a time for sharing—
and a time for remembering—
remembering the things of beauty
wasted by our careless hands—
our frequent disregard
of other living things—
the many songs unheard
because we would not listen

Listen tonight with all the wisdom
of your spirit—
listen too with all the compassion
of your heart—
lest there come another night—
when there is only silence—
A great
and
total
silence—

—Winston Abbott

98

Let sleep not come upon thy languid eyes
before each daily action thou hast scanned;
What's done amiss, what done,
what left undone;
From first to last examine all,
and then blame what is wrong;
in what is right rejoice.

—Attributed to Pythagoras

99

Every night Thou dost free our spirits
from the body's snare
and erase all impressions on the tablets
of memory.
Our spirits are set free every night
from this cage,
they are done with audience
and talk and tale.
At night prisoners forget their prison,
at night governors forget their power.
There is no sorrow,
no thought of gain or loss,
no idea of this person or that person.
Such is the state of the mystic,
even when he is not asleep:
God saith, "Thou wouldst deem them awake
while they slept."

He is asleep, day and night,
to the affairs of this world,
like a pen in the hand of the Lord.
God hath shown forth
some part of His state,
inasmuch as the vulgar too
are carried away by sleep:
Their spirits gone into
the wilderness that is beyond words,
their souls and bodies at rest.
Till with a whistle Thou callest them
back to the snare,
bringest them all again
to justice and judgment.

—RUMI

100

*The Lord almighty
grant us a quiet night
and a perfect end.*

—ANONYMOUS

101

There is great joy in darkness.
Deepen it.

—SANAI PRAYER

Identifications

All of the entries in this book come from special people or cultures, yet my aim here is to provide notes of interest on historical, rather than contemporary, personalities and cultures. In some cases, such as with the entries from indigenous cultures, it proves very difficult to find adequate background information. The inclusion of entries in this section is therefore a product of historical records.

ENTRY 2

Dag Hammarskjöld (1905–61), Swedish statesman and former United Nations secretary general, died in a plane crash over Africa. He was posthumously awarded the Nobel Peace Prize in 1961.

ENTRY 4

Shinto means "the way of the gods" in Japanese. The Shinto religion has its roots in fifth-century Japan. However, it was quickly overshadowed by Buddhism and Confucianism and did not emerge again until the eighteenth century, when it was revived as the official national religion of Japan.

ENTRIES 6, 13

The Koran, or Qur'an, is the earliest known work in Arabic prose. There are many versions known but only one authorized version, which was first published around A.D. 650. The 114 chapters of the Koran contain the Islamic religious, social, civil, commercial, military, and legal codes.

ENTRY 9

Paramahansa Yogananda was an Indian Yogi who brought his teachings to the West in the 1920s and subsequently established a center in southern California called the Self-Realization Fellowship, which is still very active today. His book *Autobiography of a Yogi* is a perennial bestseller.

ENTRY 12

Johann Wolfgang von Goethe (1749–1832) was a German poet, dramatist, novelist, and scientist. He was able to reflect his unique understanding of man's connection with nature through all of his disciplines and skills. His most famous work, *Faust*, is about a man who sells his soul to the devil in exchange for the power to cure his village of the plague.

ENTRY 15

The Atharva-Veda is the fourth in a series of ancient sacred Indian texts that were first written in Vedic, an early form of Sanskrit. This fourth Veda consists almost exclusively of hymns, magical incantations, and spells. The Vedas in their present form are believed to date from the third century B.C.

ENTRY 18

Compline is one of the nine Divine Offices, or hours, of the Roman Catholic Church. Compline is conducted every night before bedtime.

ENTRY 19

The Rig-Veda is the first of the four Vedas mentioned in Entry #14. It consists of over a thousand hymns composed in different poetic meters and separated into ten volumes.

ENTRY 24

Kekchi Maya is one of roughly twenty different languages of the Mayan tribes in Guatemala.

ENTRY 25

Sir Thomas Brown (1605–1682) was a British physician and essayist. Although sometimes considered bizarre and offbeat, his writings are full of rich imagery and an eloquence that is still highly regarded among writers of English prose.

ENTRY 33

William Laud became the archbishop of Canterbury in 1633. In 1637, he attempted to introduce the Anglican liturgy in Scotland, and a riot broke out in response. This eventually led to the First Bishops' War of 1639. He was later impeached and beheaded by the House of Commons for treason.

ENTRY 37

Nahum Bomze was a Yiddish poet and author in Europe around the turn of the twentieth century.

ENTRY 38

An antiphon is an alternate chanting or singing of a psalm or hymn by two choirs. It was introduced to the West around A.D. 500, and replaced the traditional call and response chants. For Compline, see Entry #17.

ENTRY 39

Victor Hugo (1802–85), prolific French poet, playwright, and novelist, was a primary influence on the romantic movement. His most famous work is his novel *The Hunchback of Notre Dame*, published in 1831.

ENTRY 41

The Armenian Church is easily one of the oldest branches of the Christian church, dating back to the work of the apostle St. Gregory the Illuminator, who is credited with converting King Tiridates III and several members of his court in A.D. 303.

ENTRY 43

William Blake (1757–1827) was an English poet and painter who was self-taught and heavily influenced by the works of Jakob Boehme and Emanuel Swedenborg. He died in poverty after spending his later years trying to sell his engravings.

ENTRY 45

Henry Francis Lyte (1793–1843) was a Scottish-born hymn writer who wrote many well-known hymns that are still sung today, such as "Abide with Me."

ENTRIES 49, 58

Johann Freylinghausen (1670–1739) was a hymn writer from Germany, and his *Spiritual Songbook* was instrumental in the Pietist movement.

ENTRY 51

St. Augustine (354–430), also referred to as Augustine of Hippo, was born in Algeria to pagan parents and studied several different philosophical systems prior to his Christian conversion in 387.

ENTRY 53

Western Highlanders are the clans or tribes of the Scottish high country.

ENTRY 54

Kikaku is the title given to a Japanese art school that is known for a particular style.

ENTRY 60

The Jyotiniketan community is an Indian sect that is associated with the Jain religion, which is a branch of Hinduism.

ENTRY 62

The Book of Common Prayer is the official prayer book of the Church of England as well as Anglican churches in other countries, including the Episcopal Church in America. It first appeared in 1549 during the Reformation. The most recent edition was published in 1979.

ENTRIES 67, 79

The Leonine Sacramentary is traditionally credited in part to St. Gelasius, pope from 492 to 496. This compilation of letters is believed to have been published in the sixth century.

ENTRY 69

Rabindranath Tagore (1861–1941) was an Indian-born poet, philosopher, and Nobel laureate who dedicated himself to cultural exchange between the East and West. He is considered the most popular and influential author of India's colonial era. His book *Collected Poems and Plays* was published posthumously in 1966.

ENTRY 70

John Calvin (1509–64) was a French theologian, church reformer, and humanist. The Protestant Church regarded him as a major influence on their beliefs.

ENTRIES 74, 89

Bishop Lancelot Andrewes (1555–1626) was an English theologian who took a distinctively Anglican approach to his interpretations of the Bible. He was widely regarded as one of the most learned men in England during his later years.

ENTRIES 76, 81

Rudolf Steiner (1861–1925) was an Austrian-born philosopher and scientist who founded the spiritual-scientific movement called anthroposophy. A prolific lecturer and writer, his work is still being translated and edited today, and his many initiatives, such as the Waldorf schools and biodynamic agriculture, continue to grow in popularity.

ENTRY 77

The Mozarabic liturgy was the official liturgy of the church of Spain from the sixth through the twelfth centuries. It is now found only in the Spanish city of Toledo.

ENTRY 78

Jorge Manrique was a Spanish writer during the fifteenth century, when the country was experiencing a boom in literary output. His most famous work, *Stanzas on the Death of My Father*, is about coming to terms with the death of a loved one.

ENTRY 82

Jakob Boehme (1575–1624), a German shoemaker by trade, was a passionate Christian mystic who sought direct divine illuminations. His writings and lectures appealed to both the Evangelical Church and to scientists such as Hegel and Newton, making him a true pioneer in Western metaphysical thought.

ENTRY 90

The Emperor Yang Guang ruled the Sui Dynasty in China from about 589 to 630 and is remembered in Chinese history as an emperor of self-serving ambitions. It is also believed that his many lost battles of conquest helped to hasten the fall of the Sui Dynasty.

ENTRY 91

Charles Pierre Peguy (1873–1914) was a French poet and essayist who dedicated his work to social justice and the Roman Catholic Church until he was killed at the Battle of the Marne in World War I. Other works by Peguy include *The Mystery of the Charity of Joan of Arc*, and *God Speaks*.

ENTRY 94

The song "Taps," often played at military and state funerals, has its origin with General Daniel Butterfield of the Union Army during the historic seven-days battle of the Civil War. As he was trying to bury his dead soldiers with honorary gun salutes, he repeatedly drew Confederate fire. He then sat down and wrote "Taps" for the bugler in his regiment.

ENTRY 99

Jalal al-Din Muhammad Rumi (1207–73) was a Persian mystic and poet who followed the Islamic mystical movement called Sufism. Most of his copious writings were dedicated to his spiritual master, who disappeared without a trace in 1247. The Sufi sect called the Mevlevi, or whirling dervishes, is dedicated to the writings of Rumi and remains very active today, even in the West.

Acknowledgments

Entries 48, 52, 59, and 66 from *An African Prayer Book* by Desmond Tutu. Copyright 1995 by Desmond Tutu. Used by permission of Doubleday, a division of Bantam Doubleday Dell Publishing Group, Inc.

Entries 7 and 88 from *American Indian Poetry* by George W. Cronyn. Copyright 1934 by Random House Publishing. Reprinted by permission of the publisher.

Entry 96 from *American Indian Prayers and Poetry* by J. Ed Sharpe. Copyright 1985 by Cherokee Publications, Box 256, Cherokee, North Carolina 28719. Used by permission of the publisher.

About the Editor

BRIAN WRIGHT is a writer and media producer who has been interested in spiritual development and religious practices since childhood. He lives in Minneapolis, Minnesota. He is also the editor of *Greeting the Day: Morning Prayers and Meditations from Around the World*, published by Adams Media.